TO

....

FROM

....

DATE

....

YOU ARE

God's

MASTERPIECE

60 Beautiful Reminders of
What God Says about You

STEFAN KUNZ

DaySpring
LIVE YOUR FAITH

You Are God's Masterpiece: 60 Beautiful Reminders of What God Says about You
© 2019 Stefan Kunz. All rights reserved.
First Edition, October 2019

Published by:

DaySpring

P.O. Box 1010
Siloam Springs, AR 72761
dayspring.com

Printed in China
Prime: 89904
ISBN: 978-1-68408-632-0

INTRODUCTION

Hello! I'm Stefan Kunz. I'm a letterer, designer, and freelancer who loves to find new ways to display the Word. A few years ago, I started a challenge on Instagram, inviting my fellow artists to join me in 30 Days of Bible Lettering (#30DaysBibleLettering). Every day for thirty days, we would post our lettering projects featuring nothing but Scripture. To my surprise, hundreds of people signed on, and the next thing I knew, God was spreading His love like wildfire throughout social media. In the past few years, God has really shown me that I can trust Him to take small, insignificant nothing ideas and turn them into beautiful, amazing breakthroughs. This little book is full of things I've struggled with, things I've learned, and some real-life experiences you can hopefully relate to. It's also full of truths—beautiful truths that we can all grab onto in the ups and the downs. My hope is that you'll be encouraged to keep going, keep living, knowing and trusting that you are not alone—God is with you. Whatever it is. He will never leave you.

—STEFAN KUNZ

trust in the Lord with all your Heart

PROVERBS 3:5

The LORD LOOKS AT THE HEART

When I was younger I wasn't really athletic. So when it came to picking teams, I often got picked last. It was the greatest thing ever (said no kid). It really challenged my self-worth. But that's why I love this Scripture: "Humans do not see what the LORD sees, for humans see what is visible, but the LORD sees the heart" (I Samuel 16:7 CSB).

While searching for a new king to lead His people, God chose a young shepherd boy who didn't have the same physical stature as his older brothers. But that didn't matter to God, because David was a man after His own heart. David was anointed king, fought Goliath when everyone else was too afraid, and secured a kingdom for his people. He ruled with integrity of heart. You see, when we discover how God sees us instead of how the world sees us, we can then rest in His great plans for our lives.

THE LORD IS ON my Side I WILL NOT FEAR

PSALM 118:6

You are not (or never) alone. Whatever situation you might be facing right now, know that someone is on your side, fighting with you. You don't have to fear because His love endures forever! It may seem that the whole world is working against you at any given moment. When David was facing a life-threatening situation, being viciously pursued by King Saul and his army, he chose to write, "The LORD is on my side; I will not fear" (Psalm 118:6 KJV). Keep in mind: anyone in David's position would be freaking out. Even if they know God will come through, any human who is facing an entire army coming after them is going to be frightened and nervous. However, David knew God's love is relentless. The danger of death was absolutely real, but fear is a choice. In faith, David turned to God knowing that God was for him, and if He is for us, who could be against us? (See Romans 8:31.) In the midst of all our insecurities, troubles, and fears, let's shift our focus from our problems to God and remember that He's got this. He's in control.

God can do all things more than you could ever imagine

"Now to Him who is able to do immeasurably more than all we ask or imagine, according to His power that is at work within us..." (Ephesians 3:20). It is wild to think that no matter what we pray, dream, or imagine, He can do so much more. No matter how big we dare to dream, we won't even scratch the surface of what He can do. Prayer is how we can communicate with God, at any time, roaming free and with the best reception. Jesus even gave us an example of what happens when we ask Him for something:

"Which of you, if your son asks for bread, will give him a stone? Or if he asks for a fish, will give him a snake? If you, then, though you are evil, know how to give good gifts to your children, how much more will your Father in heaven give good gifts to those who ask Him!" (Matthew 7:9–11).

I've prayed for some crazy things: losing weight fast (lost 20kg or 44lbs without trouble in five months), having my lettering displayed on Times Square (November 2018 for Coke)... And those are just two of many examples. You see, I realize that I can't dream big enough. And if He can do it for me, He can do it for you too!

BE
STRONG
AND TAKE
HEART

PSALM 27:14

When you're in a battle—whether it be illness, a family dispute, or negative thoughts—it's a lot harder to give up when you know help is on its way. While we might be staring our enemies in the eyes, it's easier to fight with all we have because we know that God is bigger than anything. And we know that He is going to show up at just the right moment.

In the meantime, we just need to give it all we've got and fight the best we can. Our job is to lean on His strength and take heart! He is coming to our rescue. We can trust that.

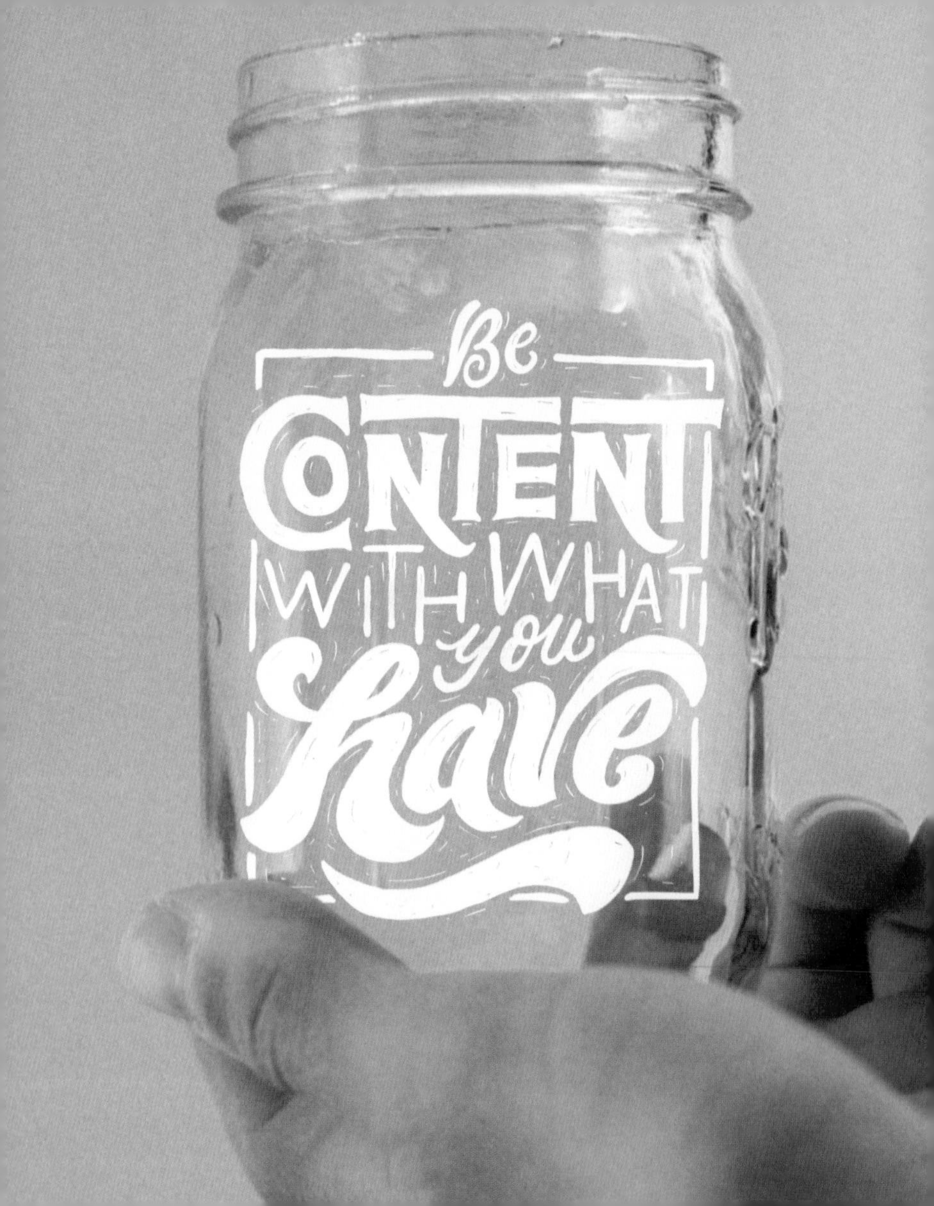
Be
CONTENT
WITH WHAT
you
have

When you look at this picture, what do you see? A jar filled to the rim with…nothing? Take a closer look. It's not nothing—it's an empty jar, which can be used in so many different ways. You can store homemade jam, make tea light holders, serve milkshakes, or even create snow globes with empty jars. But, you saw "nothing."

Have you been disregarding the skills, gifts, and tools that God gave you? When you offer everything you have to the Lord, and I mean everything—from your kitchen pans to your talents to your hands and feet—you'll see that He will fill them. He will show you how to use your God-given abilities and strengths to create big things out of nothing.

Don't Forget to Do Good

HEBREWS 13:16

It's so easy to believe that we don't have the power or authority to create change. We see authority figures making big changes and we think to ourselves: *They're taking care of it. I'll just go about my business and leave it to them.* But we couldn't be more wrong! Every single person on this planet can make a difference. We can accomplish so much with small acts of kindness. And when all of these small acts start adding up, not even the person who holds the highest office in all the land can compare to the power of a collective kindness.

We may not always be able to make big, elaborate things happen on a daily basis, but we can say thank you for services rendered, pay for a stranger's coffee, and encourage a child with a compliment like "good job!" With each small act of kindness, we can share God's love and make a difference in at least one person's life every single day. And this will make a difference in our lives too.

Have you ever brought a beautiful plant home only to have it slowly wither away one leaf at a time? This usually doesn't happen overnight, right? It's a slow process and let's face it, the end result is usually due to continual neglect.

Here's a tip: the key to maintaining a healthy plant is keeping its root system strong. Plants need care, water, and sun to grow. And it's no different when it comes to humans! When we spend time with God, talking to Him and letting Him pour into us, we develop a strong root system—a foundation that results in a supernatural strength and an indescribable peace.

So, pray as if it's your sunlight, talk to God (even yell if you need to get His attention), and drink in the Bible like it's pouring water over you. In the same way the sun doesn't need plants, God doesn't need our prayers, but He wants them because He wants to shower us with His goodness. So why not let Him?

The beginning of every year stresses me out. It usually starts slow and I feel behind on my goals and what I want to achieve. I start to take matters into my own hands and act. But that just stresses me even more and I forget to breathe, relax, and trust the One who has always taken care of me—the One who has been with me every year of my life without exception.

And yet, there's more! God is going to continue to take care of me. He has great plans for me. There is so much to look forward to. I just need to keep calm, trust God, and know He's got this.

Whatever is stressing you out right now, take a deep breath, maybe two or as many as you need. Think of it like this: You're rowing your boat against a stiff breeze. There is lots of effort with little progress. But now imagine you are in a sailboat. You don't have to work to get anywhere. You relax and let the wind take you on a pleasant journey. We can trust His journey is going to be amazing.

My main goal in life is to become more and more like Jesus. And for that to happen, I need to make more room for Him and less room for me. Because, let's face it—I tend to think about myself quite a bit. I think about my circumstances, my future, my projects, my goals—and when my thoughts are on me, there's really no room for Him.

And the thing is: God is limitless. So why am I focusing on myself when I could rely on His strength to see me through all of it? To take me further than I could ever imagine going on my own?

What is it that you have given up on? What is it that you thought was just too crazy to keep praying for? Don't give up. Release your unbelief to Him and watch Him turn the impossible into possible.

'Love' endures all things

Have you ever gone on a long road trip with someone you knew? If you haven't, let me tell you, it can be quite intense. You spend pretty much every minute with each other, and the person you thought you knew somehow appears different. Suddenly little things you once overlooked, like chewing loudly, become monsters and get really annoying.

Love doesn't work on changing people, it accepts others and loves them the way they are. Even if the chewing can be measured in decibels, love endures it all.

God's love is greater than anyone can imagine. We think to ourselves: If God knows my innermost scars, my crazy thoughts, and my annoying little habits, there's no way He could ever love me. He's probably so over me. But, the truth is: God is love. His love always protects, always trusts, always hopes, and always perseveres—no matter how loud our chewing is.

What are you most afraid of? Losing a loved one? Getting sick? Making ends meet?

In a not-so-famous Will Smith movie, one of his lines was, "Danger is real, fear is a choice." In other words, we are responsible for how we deal with danger. Easier said than done, right?

I, for one, am afraid of heights so I simply choose to avoid rooftops and roller coasters. However, as a freelancer, I am dependent on projects coming my way, and when they don't seem to be rolling in, it can lead me down a path of severe worry and fret. It's a fear I can't simply avoid. It's during these times that I constantly need to put my trust in God. Because He has always provided, and He always will.

We can't do everything to perfection and that's okay. It's called being human. But accepting this simple fact is actually really hard. We feel that we have to fulfill our own and others' expectations. Some often put it this way, "You need to be good and do _____ " to be accepted. However, Jesus doesn't come with an expectation but an invitation: "Come to me, all of you who are weary and burdened, and I will give you rest" (Matthew 11:28 CSB).

Keeping the peace is hard to do.

In a world full of differing opinions, never-ending conflicts, and senseless hatred, it's crazy to think that peace is even possible, right? But Philippians 4:7 (CSB) tells us, "The peace of God, which surpasses all understanding, will guard your hearts and minds in Christ Jesus." So if we ask Him to guard our hearts and minds, and if we ask Him to give us the tools to pursue peace, then maybe, just maybe we can live in peace and be peacemakers for the people around us. Wouldn't that be worth asking for?

Remember THE things I HAVE DONE IN THE Past

God has great plans for us. At times He even tells us about them and gives a promise like He gave Abraham, Joseph, and David. But then comes the period of time between the promise and the fulfillment. While waiting, we must remember who He is and what He has already done. Every experience He's given us, every person He's placed in our lives are the perfect preparation for a future that only He can create. When has He ever disappointed us? The answer is never. So why would we think that now? God's got us, even when it doesn't feel like it. He is the God who can and will move mountains on our behalf. He does have a plan for everyone and everything. Be patient and wait for the plan to fall into place in His perfect timing.

ISAIAH 46:9 NLT

LET US
RUN
THE
Race
WITH
ENDURANCE
THAT -IS- SET
Before
US
HEBREWS 12:1
LEAD ME INTO ALL TRUTH
PILOT

Have you ever known a runner? One who trains for marathons? Runs long distances?

There is a lot more to it than one would imagine. Runners actually prepare for their race by eating the right foods, getting the right gear, maintaining a strict running schedule, staying lean (no weight lifting), and cross-training. All so they can achieve success at the finish line.

In life, we're told that the race before us should be filled with perseverance, much fruit, and good stories. But most people forget the part of the Bible verse that is written right before the much-loved Scripture: "Let us run with endurance the race that is set before us" (Hebrews 12:1 ESV). They forget the part that says to "lay aside every weight, and sin which clings so closely" (verse 1). What is stopping you from running the race? What is weighing you down? Past experience, failure, shame? Whatever it is, start by trusting God with it and take the weight off your shoulders. You'll see, the more you let go the lighter you get and the longer you can run.

HEBREWS 12:1 PARAPHRASED

What happens when we don't feel like rejoicing? Are we supposed to rejoice no matter what circumstances we face? And in all reality, is this even really possible?

In the Bible, Paul writes a handful of letters from prison (some under house arrest), and in these letters, he is always joyful. In Acts, we find that Paul actually sings while he is behind bars. Now, that's rejoicing on another level! Although he was imprisoned, Paul didn't let his mind wander to the dark places, but he focused on the why and how much success he was having with his mission.

Isn't that an incredibly valuable lesson? Just imagine: what would happen if we focused on the why—the mission rather than the circumstances we find ourselves in today?

PHILIPPIANS 4:4 KJV

LOVE IS PATIENT

1. CORINTHIANS 13,4

God's love isn't selfish; it's not in a hurry; it waits for us. His love for us is immensely patient—we mess up again and again, but He still loves us. He wants the best for us, and He is cheering us on, whether it's our first attempt or our thirty-ninth. That kind of love, the Fatherly love He has for us, is the love we need to share with others. When people mess up (and they will), when they are late again (and they will be), let's be sure to give them the love our God gives us, the patient, unselfish, not-in-a-hurry kind of love.

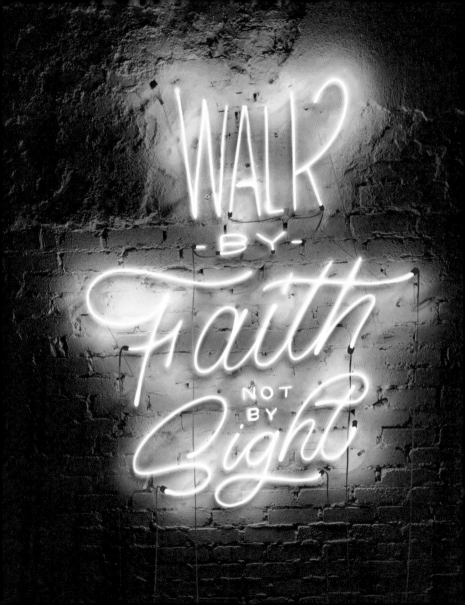

Ever had to walk home in the middle of the night and all you had was your phone's flashlight? I have, on multiple occasions. I could barely see where to put one foot in front of the other, but you know what? That's all I needed, and it got me home. To walk by faith is very similar. Trusting God is risky, exciting, and, at times, unsettling. When we start on the journey, all we are shown is the first step. Abraham left his home with a promise, not sure exactly where he would end his journey. David faced a giant carrying a few stones and a slingshot. Noah built an ark on dry land long before the rain began.

Once we take the first step into the unknown, we can trust that He will fill in the details as we move forward. When we walk in faith, we put our trust in His promise (found in Psalm 23) to lead us to green pastures and refreshing waters. We can be sure we are in good hands.

Why? Why do we do things we know we're going to regret? Whether it's staying up late to binge watch our favorite television show or putting off an important project until the very last minute, we know these actions are only going to hurt us in the long run. And the next day, our future self has to deal with the consequences. There are plenty of examples of procrastination when it comes to choosing a better lifestyle...a better future. We would rather deal with change "tomorrow" than choose to fight for change "today." However, it's our future we are talking about here! It's a life choice that is worth fighting for because it will create a better future for us physically, emotionally, and spiritually. It's entirely up to us to fight for change now. Where will we start?

BUT I
TRUST
IN YOUR
LOVE
Unfailing

I don't know about you, but sometimes I go through hard times and have moments when I wonder if God is really there. During these times, I will ask God how long my trial will last. And as I wait on Him to answer my prayer, I secretly wonder if He heard me. Then I start to wrestle with doubt, sorrow, and fear as I anxiously await His answer. At times like this, it helps if I remind myself that I can rest in His unfailing love.

He is bigger than my circumstances. He is bigger than my doubt. He loves me with an unconditional, unimaginable love—the kind that overcomes any doubts or fears I may be facing. And, He is bigger than anything you are facing too!

BE

STRONG

IN THE

Lord

Have you ever had a friend who was much stronger than you? Growing up, I wasn't the strong kid. I actually got bullied a lot. I always wished for a friend twice the size of me who would have my back—someone I could rely on when the situation turned bad.

We often face difficulties in life where we need to be strong to get through them, but at the same time our strength is limited. How great is it, though, that in those situations, we can rely not on our own strength but on His. Yes, a God so mighty there's no situation out of His control. We are safe with Him! And we can be strong and face whatever comes our way. Amazing things happen when we lean on God's strength and stop relying on our own.

EPHESIANS 6:10 KJV

TRUST IN THE LORD WITH ALL YOUR HEART

PROVERBS 3:5

In life, there are ups and downs of all sorts. But if we trust—and I mean fully trust—in God with all our hearts and minds, then we can live in the confidence of knowing that no matter what problems come our way, they will all be solved.

Plus, if we believe He is for us—that the King of the world is in our corner—we might just find that extraordinary things will start to happen. We might just start recognizing Him in all aspects of our lives, in good times and bad…happy moments and sad. So no matter what season of life you're currently in, whether it be smooth sails or rocky waters, place your trust in Him. You can trust that He will answer. Believe it with all your heart.

In PE class, were you ever the first pick? I wasn't. Actually, as a chubby kid, I usually was the last. I hated that. I always felt overlooked. But imagine if the president came up to you and said these words: "You are chosen." Wouldn't that make your day or year?

Well, God thought of you before you were born and made you the way you are. Each little detail wasn't an accident; it was a choice. He has a beautiful plan for your life and wants what is best for you because He loves you.

WE ARE BETTER TOGETHER! Imagine yourself running a race with people on the left and right of you holding signs, screaming your name, clapping and cheering as you pass by. This can totally boost your energy and help you get to the finish line. That's why I love to encourage others and cheer them on, because I know that more often than not, it can and will help them reach their goal. Take today as an opportunity to cheer someone on; encourage them in what they are doing.

LOVED you AT YOUR DARKEST

You are loved, no matter what! When you think of your darkest, most shameful moment, do you feel God's love with you? It's hard to believe, but He is loving you even in that place.

God loves you despite anything you've done. If He wanted to condemn you for your actions, He would have sent a judge, but He sent a Savior. He sent you Someone to take your place and take that shame away so you can be free. He loved you at your darkest.

When the cares of my heart are many,
your consolations cheer my soul.
PSALM 94:19 ESV

When I was going through a personal crisis, I went on a lot of walks where I would cry my heart out to God. I no longer knew what else to do. My friends—even though they meant well—gave me tons of advice on what I should and shouldn't do. But on those walks, I felt like God was listening to my cries, consoling me, and that's what my soul needed most. Maybe you are in a similar situation, not needing advice but Someone who will listen to you and be there to console you.

Remember: You can take everything to God in prayer. Cry out to Him if you need to. Be loud and real and let it all out. He can take it. He knows your heart, and He's ready to walk with you.

At one point or another, we've all felt as if God couldn't possibly love us. We've asked ourselves questions like, *How could He love me after I did that?* We think: *There's no possible way God will ever forgive me for that.* But there's good news: God's love is not based on any merit or achievement, ability or looks. He simply loves us. To demonstrate His love, He made the ultimate sacrifice, paying the price by giving His life for ours. His love touches our past with forgiveness, gives meaning to our present, and secures our future. God loves us because God is love, not because of who we are. It really is that simple.

I JOHN 4:19

Waiting for God is grueling at times, especially when you feel stuck. It just seems like God is taking forever so you jump the gun, make a move, and decide to start moving. Unfortunately, every time I've done this in my life, it's only ended in regret. But do you know what comes out of regret? Wisdom.

Mistakes and regrets teach us about life and make us who we are. We learn from them and move on. And next time, I'll wait for His nudge before I act.

What is it that guides us day to day? Is it intuition or wisdom? Or is it God's Spirit? In our choices, do we choose the path of least resistance or do we climb the mountain that is in front of us? The path of our life does boil down to the decisions we make. We can choose to trust the One who knows infinitely more than we do.

We know that His intentions for us are only good. He is loving and faithful, and we can let go and follow His path filled with true wisdom. That is the faith that moves mountains.

PSALM 143:10

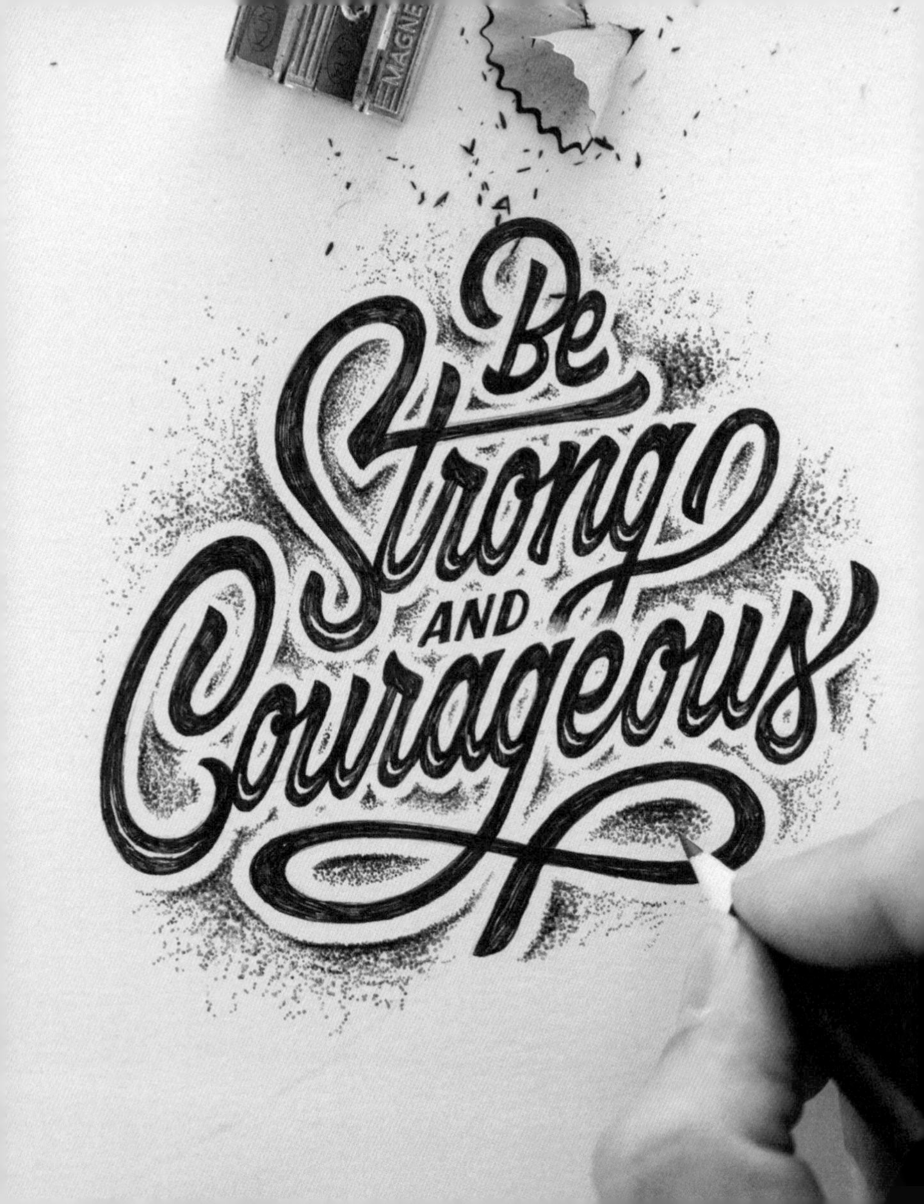
Be
Strong
AND
Courageous

Ever wondered what your life would look like if you were never afraid of anything? What would it look like if you were always strong and courageous? Just imagine how different you would approach each challenge...you would just walk right up to it and do it.

I can't tell you how scared I was to start an Instagram campaign called #30daysofbiblelettering. I felt like the extra challenge would and could boil everything over. I was mostly scared because I felt like I couldn't come up with any more good ideas, and signing on to come up with thirty new ones every day for thirty days sounded crazy. But since I felt that God had placed this challenge on my heart, I relied more on Him to give me the strength and go with me, just as He promised Joshua and all of us. Yes, that includes you too! So next time the challenge seems crazy, remember to lean on God's strength and go for it!

LOVE your LIFE

Youthfull IN Spirit · GENEROUS at ➤ Heart · Fac
CO

Seek the Lord while He may be found;
call to Him while He is near.
ISAIAH 55:6 CSB

I was visiting Bali, Indonesia, when the Mount Agung volcano decided to erupt, spewing a massive ash plume two kilometers into the sky. It was crazy. Fortunately, I was safe at a friend's house and didn't have to evacuate. But the airport closed so I was stuck for four days trying to find a flight out of there. Needless to say, I was frustrated. I even started driving to a different airport twelve hours away before I received the news that the airport in Bali had reopened. So I turned around to go back to the Bali airport only to find out I didn't have a seat on any of the flights going out. That's when I lost it. I went back to my room and lost it—I screamed to God and told Him everything that was on my mind. I woke up the next morning to a booked flight and made it back home safely that day.

You see, God answered my prayer even though it came out in the form of screams. He didn't mind that I was frustrated; He understood my heart and my need even more than I did. He loves it when we call out to Him. He's a big God, and we can call to Him whenever, however, and wherever we are. There is absolutely power in prayer.

ROMANS 10:13 KJV

GOD IS OUR REFUGE AND STRENGTH AN EVER PRESENT HELP IN TROUBLE

PSALM 46:1

What do you do when you find yourself in a little trouble? Do you call someone for help or try to solve the problem yourself? I'm definitely the latter, too proud to ask others for help. I tell myself: *Why should someone else be able to help me if I can't do it myself?* Then I get a little further into the project and realize: *Maybe I should have taken them up on their offer to help me.* Then there's the awkward moment of going back to the one who offered to help, head down in shame, and admitting that you did need their help after all.

Well, you don't have to feel ashamed! God is like a Father who wants His children to succeed. He never gloats over our problems. He wants to help us in every situation. I am still learning to go to Him faster and waste less time trying to fix it on my own. He is our strength and refuge whenever we need it.

You're my everything

God is my everything. He never leaves me. When I am completely depleted, He fills me back up. I depend on Him for every breath. When life is hard, His arms are wide open. He holds me with His love and makes all things new. I don't know about you, but I don't want to live a day without Him. He is my everything. Period.

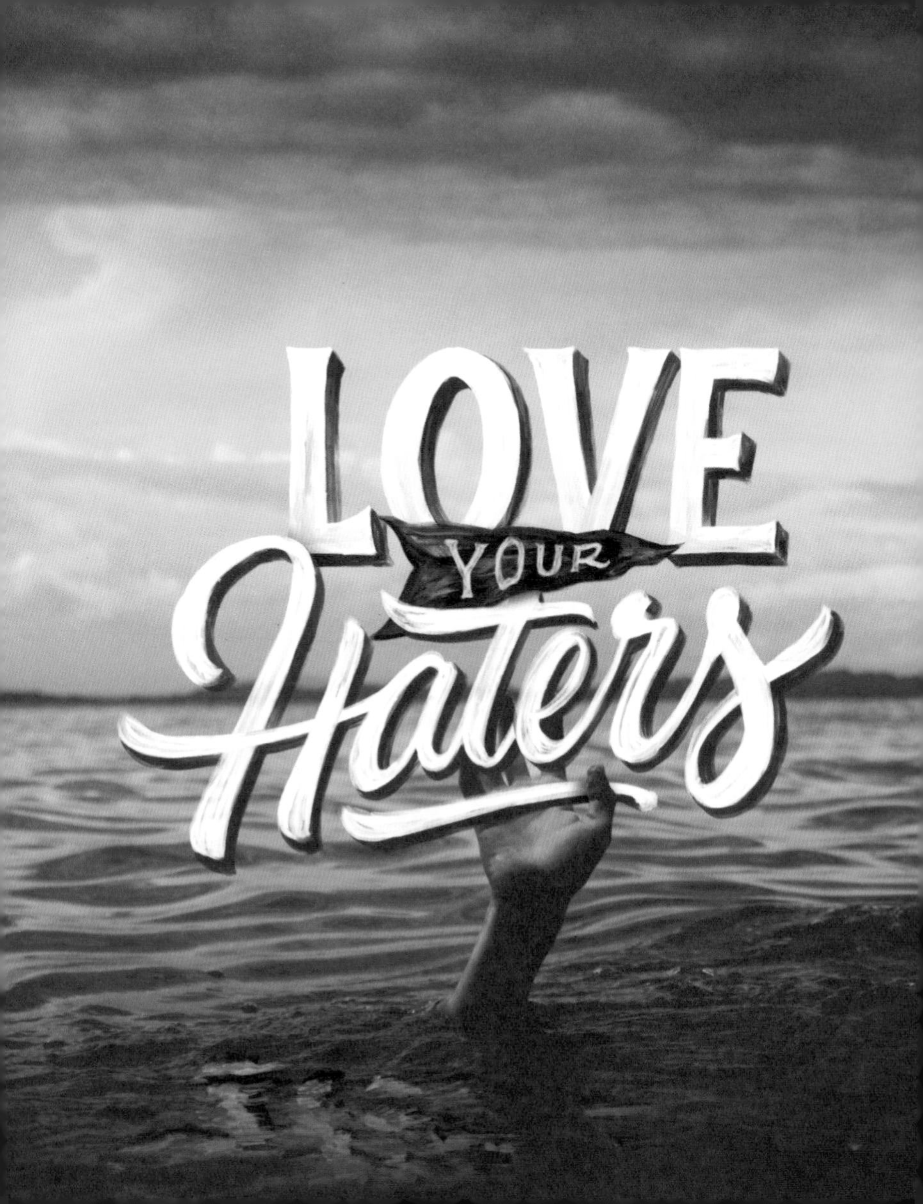
LOVE
YOUR
Haters

I was driving home from church one day when the car in front of me blocked me from leaving because it was in the wrong lane at the red light. I know this wouldn't bother you, but man, I almost lost it and wished the driver all kind of things.

Then I remembered God's love. I mean, Jesus took LOVE to a whole new level. "Love your enemies and pray for those who persecute you" (Matthew 5:44). Jesus didn't just talk the talk; He also walked the walk. He didn't only die for us but prayed for and forgave those who nailed Him to that cross.

Man, I was angry out of my mind at that driver. And all he did was block me for a few minutes. But that's where I can start. Where can you start and whom could you pray for?

HEAVEN CLOSER IS SER THAN YOU KNOW

It's easy to sign on to the idea of climbing the ladder, setting standards and achieving goals, getting better and better with every step, making it closer and closer to heaven. But if you're not careful, this idea can be a trap.

Think about it: When Jesus came to earth, He met the ones living closest to the ground, He loved on the ones who were broken in pieces, and He took time to sit with the ones who seemingly had nothing. It's nice to have my ducks in a row, but it's often when I have nothing else left and I let go of the masks and step down from the pedestal I built for myself that I feel closest to heaven. That's when I can enjoy and accept who I am, who He made me to be.

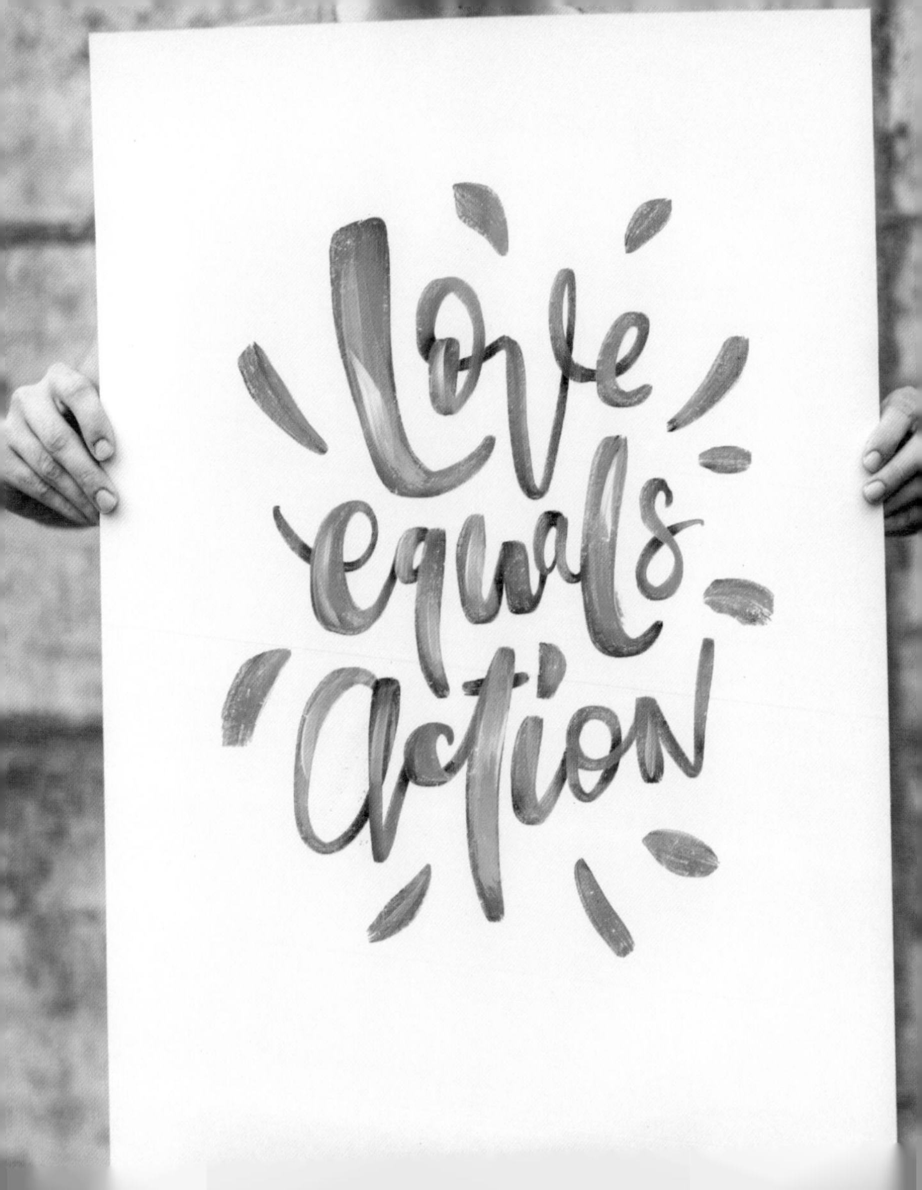
Love
equals
action

I try to show love in every single thing I do.

We've all heard the saying, "Actions speak louder than words." Love shows itself in the things we say and do. It is seen in the way we treat other people. We experience love in action in the hug of a child, concern for a friend, and even in the joy of a pet. Yet, true love is constant. It is not a mere emotion. We know that "love bears all things, believes all things, hopes all things, endures all things" (I Corinthians 13:7 ESV). So love goes beyond a simple emotion to a passion that cares for others in good times and bad, happy times and sad.

THE
Lord
HIMSELF
WILL
FIGHT
FOR YOU

EXODUS 14:14

Even when storms rage or the world around you caves, KNOW that HE IS GREATER and HE IS FIGHTING FOR YOU. In fact, He makes our fights His own. Every time I feel like I'm in a battle, I remember this and it immediately calms my nerves. And I'm able to let go of the fight because I know He'll take it from here. I don't have to struggle.

God is greater than whatever you may face. So be still, trust, and leave the battle to Him. Have faith, not fear. Rest up—He's got your back.

EXODUS 14:14 NLT

What are you afraid of? Maybe someone told you pursuing a creative career isn't a good decision, or maybe they said you were too young or even too old to start something new. Don't listen to them. Even if it scares you a little, there is no better time than today to try it out. Go for it!

Place your faith in the Giver of dreams. Hasn't He taken care of you so far? You can trust Him to lead you step-by-step toward your God-given dreams. Good things do come to those who believe, and the best things come to those who don't give up. You got this!

Don't give up! Don't get tired of doing good! Look around you—it helps to get inspired by others, see the good others are doing, and ask yourself, *What can I do today?*

And the good news is that it doesn't have to be a monumental work. Just plant seeds. Every seed is watered by God, and in His timing, not our own, we will reap a harvest.

Let's change this world and do good to all people!

I didn't exactly fit in at school. Let's just say I never was what they called "popular." I tried, but I found the more effort I gave to being someone I wasn't, the more I lost sight of how truly amazing God can be.

It is in my DNA to be creative. When I tap into that, I find that the Creator wants me to be passionate about stepping beyond normal to seeking out the extraordinary He has planned for me. Does He do the same for you? We can dare to have great expectations and to believe in them. We can be what He created us to be. And we can be inspired by His masterpieces to bring our artwork to life.

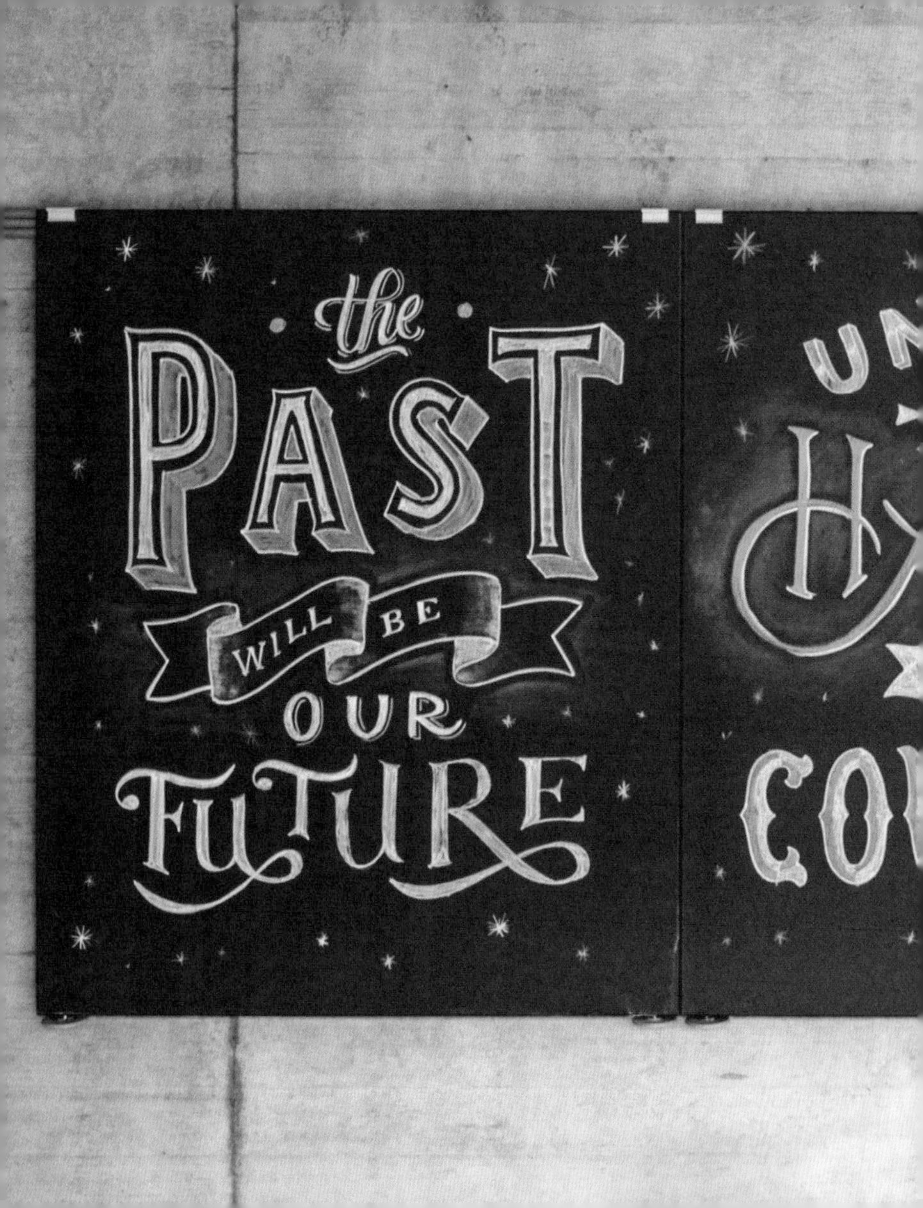
the
PAST
WILL BE
OUR
FUTURE

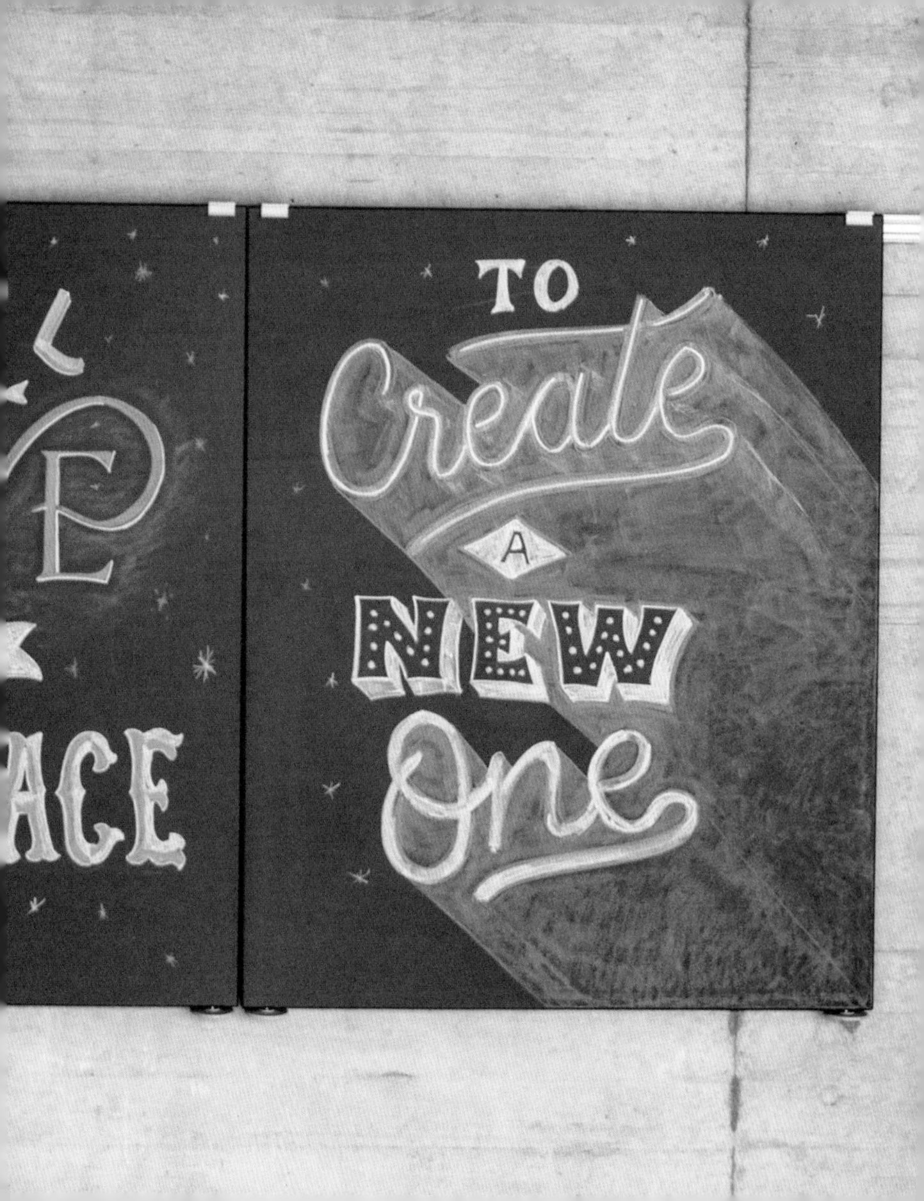
ACE
TO
Create
A
NEW
One

When
YOU GO
THROUGH
DEEP
DEEP
Waters
I WILL BE
WITH YOU

If I were to tell you that life is only sunshine and rainbows, that would be a lie. You may find yourself in the middle of a storm, just coming out of one, or, sadly, about to enter one. It looks like we cannot avoid them.

But there is GOOD NEWS! You don't have to go through the storms alone. No matter what circumstances you are facing, our heavenly Father is always there and will always face them with you. I honestly hate storms, but I wouldn't be where I am today without having gone through every single one of them. I still carry some scars, don't get me wrong. Some of them haven't even fully healed yet. Actually, I remember the worst time of my life when the storm was raging like a hurricane not for days or weeks, but for months. It was my hardest battle, but God encouraged me with His words: "Don't be afraid, for I am with you" (Isaiah 41:10 NLT). By taking my hand and walking me through it one step at a time, God helped me through that season.

He will do the same for you. YOU ARE NOT ALONE. Don't be afraid to reach out and ask for help!

ISAIAH 43:2 NLT

DONE IS Better THAN PERFECT

The struggle is real. I'll start a project with an end in mind. Then I'll get interrupted, bored, or discouraged and think that it is not perfect and put it to the side. I'll give up.

But the hard truth is, each project is not going to reach perfection, but it can reach completion. And honestly, while I may see the flaws in my work, others really don't. Perfection may be the goal, but completion moves me forward.

I hate cleaning my room. When I was younger, my mom often asked me to clean my messy room. My room was a disaster, probably because I was great at tidying by hiding my mess under my bed or closet. (To my future kids: I'll find eeeeeverything!) You can imagine that at some point my room had to burst and I couldn't hide any longer. I had to go through every corner and leave no laundry pile unturned.

Life isn't that different—it gets messy, and whatever you don't address can turn into a nasty habit or something you'll have a hard time getting rid of later. It can be an unhealthy relationship or obsession, a habit of distorting the truth, or many other things. And like cleaning your room, it's so much easier if someone comes and offers to help. That's the Holy Spirit, the Helper, who is so keen to step into our mess and turn it into something beautiful. This is what you should know about Him:

1. He's a gentleman and won't force Himself on you, but He is always there, ready to help.
2. He'll never judge you, no matter the mess you are in.
3. He doesn't do quick fixes. He goes through every corner and makes sure you don't miss a spot.

So, why wouldn't you accept His help?

COMMIT YOURSELF TO THE LORD AND HE WILL ESTABLISH YOUR PLANS

PSALM 37:5

I don't know where I am going, but I trust the One guiding me. Years ago, I made the decision to embark on an adventure and follow Jesus. It's been the best and craziest decision I've ever made that has led me to where I am today! I couldn't have dreamed it even if I wanted to. To be a full-time artist and travel around the world, getting to inspire and encourage people—seriously, it's a dream. But I had to learn to let go of my own plans. I had to stop pursuing certain clients and projects and instead follow the opportunities that God opened up for me. Once I stopped trying to run the other way, He showed up and led me to the right path. (Note: He never holds you back.)

I am so thankful, and I want to do the best that I can but let Him lead the way. For His ways are higher and better. So I hold on to Him and the best possible future. What do you need to stop pursuing? What do you need to let go of in order to make room for God's amazing plan for your life?

PSALM 37:5 PARAPHRASED

Make
FAILURE
Part
OF
your
PROCESS

Avoiding failure often results in failing to try altogether. We give up before we even get started. Greatness doesn't come from not making mistakes but learning lessons from them. So don't be afraid of making them; be afraid of not even trying. Get uncomfortable—it's okay!

Don't worry about potential failures; worry about what will be missed if you never try something new. Taking the first step in the adventure is moving toward a bright, successful future.

Faith IS THE ASSURANCE OF Things HOPED FOR

Relax is not a word in my vocabulary. I tend to get stressed out over things I can't control, like how many freelance projects I'll get next month. Will there be enough to make ends meet? I get worried, anxious, and frustrated. And I find it hard to trust God. And yet—God blows my mind every time. He is my agent and He will open the doors at the right time.

What are you stressed about? Even though you may not be able to see Him, God is at work in your life. The path of faith may be filled with delays, doubts, and moments of weakness. However, I'm learning every day to put His desires first, trust in His timing, and continue to believe in the promise until the miracle happens. And it's not *if* the miracle happens but *when*.

HEBREWS 11:1 ESV

Do your dreams scare you? Mine do. I dream up some crazy things like being a guest on a late-night talk show, flying on a private jet, landing a million-dollar deal—just to name a few.

As much as it would like to, fear isn't going to stop me from attempting the near impossible—and you shouldn't let it stop you either. God can do more than we could ever dream or imagine. Remember that! It may not be easy. We may have to take two steps forward and one step backward along the way. But crazy dreams don't scare God, so they don't scare me either.

I've found that I go further in life when I'm walking with people who believe in me, the people who support me, encourage me, and tell me when I've lost my mind. Why? Because we are better together! It's important to surround yourself with people who inspire you to do better and go further. And it's just as important to be an inspiration and an encourager to someone else. It's so important!

As humans, we will face many challenges in life, and yes, we will occasionally stumble along the way. But when we walk together, we will not fall; we will not be defeated. We can live boldly together—through the ups and downs—because together is just a good place to be.

WEEPING MAY Endure FOR A NIGHT BUT Joy COMES IN THE MORNING

Fill in the blank: It's the most _____ time of the year!

For many of us, the holidays are actually anything but wonderful. Years ago, around Christmas, I was going through the absolute worst time of my life, and the worst part was, I didn't feel like it would ever end. Every day was a battle.

How good it is to know that God is fighting our battles with us and promising us that the weeping may endure for a night but joy comes in the morning (Psalm 30:5). If you are in such a season, hold on to that promise. The night will pass and the morning will come. Don't ever give up. And be brave enough to ask for help.

Did you know that planting a tulip between rocks is not very smart? It might look great, but that's not a great environment. The plant will not flourish to its full potential. We're not that different. We need to be planted in a great environment. We need to be firmly rooted in Jesus in order to grow and flourish. We need to be centered in Him in order for Him to use us in amazing ways—exciting, new, and fresh ways, ways we would never even imagine.

Abide, Jesus says. *Remain. Dwell. Be centered. Have roots in Me.*

BLESSED IS THE One WHO TRU

WHOSE CONFIDENCE IS IN

They WILL BE LIKE A TREE Plante

IN THE Lord

THE

WATER

JEREMIAH 17:7

GRATITUDE TURNS *we* WHAT HAVE INTO ENOUGH

When will we ever have enough? Right now, your enough could look like paying your bills, buying your groceries, or owning a house, but what then?

Let's face it, we live in a world consumed by a desire for more. We are caught in a cycle that tells us if we have this, then we'll have enough, we'll be fulfilled. We can break out of this cycle by being thankful for what we already have, rather than focusing on what we wish we had. We can start by counting all the blessings we have, including friendships, health, and even our material goods. This helps us practice gratitude and reminds us to see what we do have rather than what we don't.

But SEEK First The Kingdom of God

MATTHEW 6:33

But seek first the kingdom of God and his righteousness,
and all these things will be added to you.
MATTHEW 6:33 ESV

As I was reading today's verse, I couldn't help but read the full passage to get context (which I should do anyways). In this passage, Jesus tells us a lot about how to live. How to pray and how to not worry... And what strikes me is how our instinct is to look out for ourselves and try to solve all our problems. But over a long period of time I've learned (but keep forgetting) there are rules as undeniable as gravity, such as tithing. To give is better than to receive. Not that receiving is bad, but there is a greater blessing in giving.

And if you seek first the kingdom of God and His righteousness, He will give you the desires of your heart. And that's exactly what I have experienced in the last year since I quit my job at the bank and moved to self-employment. God has been good all along, and trusting Him and putting Him first has led me to where I am today. I hope this inspires and encourages you.

MATTHEW 6:33 ESV

the LORD is my Shepherd I shall not want

psalm 23:1

The Lord is our Shepherd. He watches over us. He makes plans for us. He walks with us. He guides us and protects us. And He does it with a gentleness, an easiness, a lovingness.

As sheep, we rely on our Shepherd. When we listen to His voice, He leads us to green pastures. When we face difficulties, He leads us to quiet waters. When we wander down a dark path, He seeks us out and comforts us. As sheep, we need and rely on the Shepherd for all we face in life. Because God is a Good Shepherd, He will ensure we have everything we need.

PSALM 23:1 KJV

You can't change the past, so why give it room to consume your present and future? Let's not spend this year thinking about last year but rather create the future we want for ourselves. There are more opportunities to be encountered, achievements to be made, milestones to be reached, and goals to be scored. I don't know what the future will look like for me or for you and it might be full of uncertainties, but what I do know is that God has a plan for every single one of us. So I want to trust Him more.

THERE IS ALWAYS SOMETHING TO BE THANKFUL FOR

Every morning I wake up, smile, jump to my feet, and...NOPE, that's not me. I am rarely thankful for anything in the morning before I get my coffee. But if you think about it, I have a lot of stuff to be thankful for between the time I wake up and the time I get my coffee. For instance, to make coffee I have to have running water, electricity, a coffee machine, coffee beans, milk, and my beautiful, comfy chair. That's six things! Six cool things I could be grateful for, yet I totally miss them in my mission for coffee.

What are you looking forward to today? What are some steps in between that you could be thankful for?

The threatening buzz of a mosquito makes me jump to my feet and turns me into a hunter. I'll stay up all night doing whatever it takes to kill this tiny insect. One night in particular I was throwing blankets, turning over cushions, and inspecting every corner when I came to the conclusion that the bug must have vanished. So I turned the lights off, got back in bed, closed my eyes, and as soon as I started dozing off…bzzzzzzzzzzz. It was a long night. In the end, two mosquitos were harmed in the process. And I have zero regrets about this.

But talking about making a difference, the size of your influence doesn't matter. The way you live your life speaks louder than words could ever preach. One act of kindness can inspire two others, and before you know it, you've inspired the whole world. Let's be the difference we want to see in the world!

IF YOU DONT
BELIEVE
IN
Miracles
PERHAPS
YOU'VE
FORGOTTEN
you are
ONE

How many of us wake up every morning and immediately think, *I'm a miracle! I'm awesome!* Not me. And I certainly don't know anyone who does. Why would we? I mean, it is just another day.

What would happen, though, if we did take a few moments every morning to remember that we were made with a specific purpose in mind? It could change our whole day. What if we set aside time each day to focus on the fact that we were fearfully and wonderfully made, that we were created as valuable beings, needed in the world today? After all, God does not make mistakes. He makes miracles. We should know. Each and every one of us is one.

THAT THE

Works

OF

God

MIGHT BE

DISPLAYED

IN

HIM

Do you remember the darkest days of your life? Did you secretly ask yourself why He, the perfect, almighty God, would allow something so imperfect to happen?

It's in times like these that I trust God sees the bigger picture. And I trust that He will turn my suffering into something great— something that He can still use and weave into His beautiful plan. Unfortunately, I don't get to see His plan right now. Sometimes it takes years for God to reveal why I struggled the way I did, and sometimes I don't ever get to know.

But, it is so good to know that God has a plan for all things— the beautiful things, the painful things, the exciting things, the lovely things, and the broken things. It is good to know that "in all things God works for the good of those who love Him" (Romans 8:28). It's just good to know and be able to trust that.

JOHN 9:3

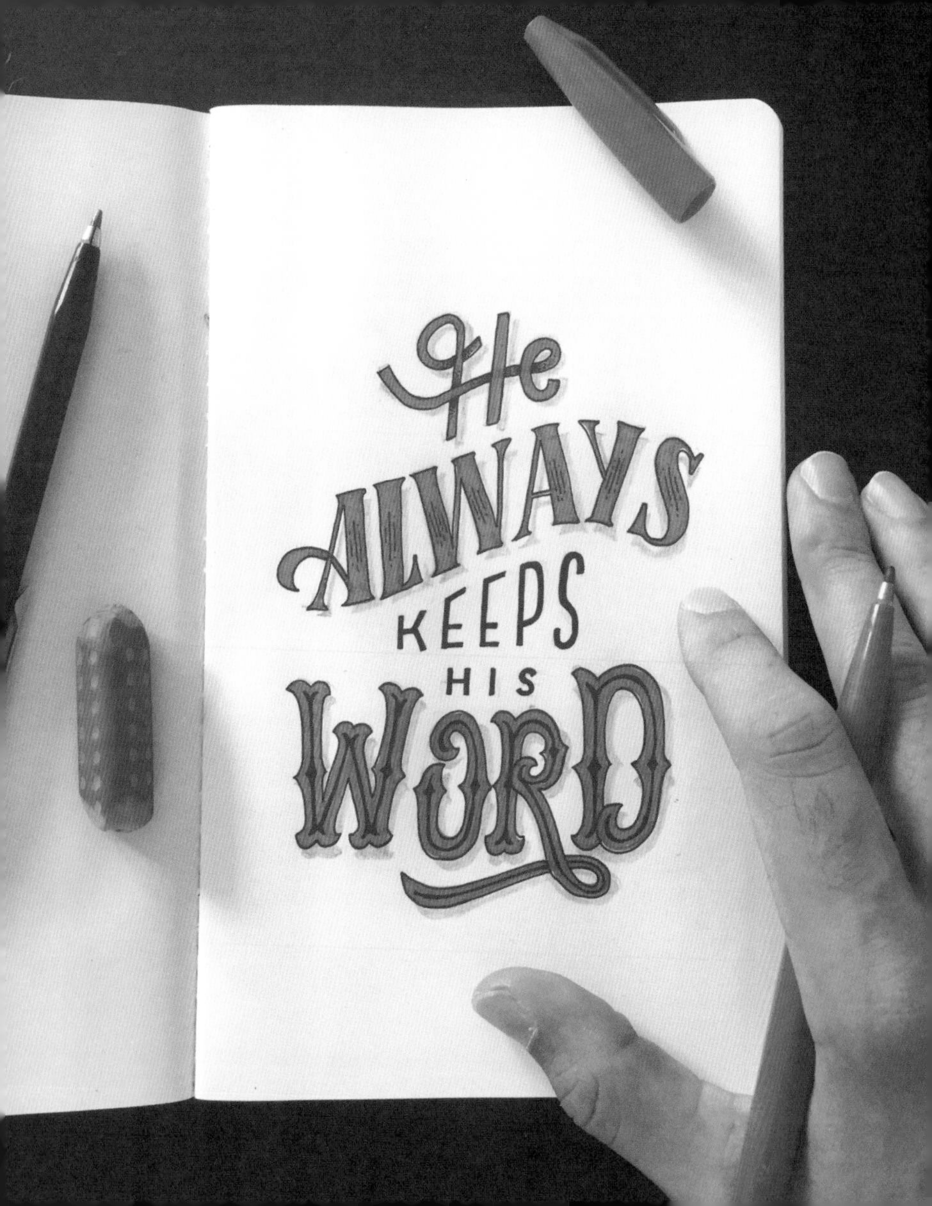
He
ALWAYS
KEEPS
HIS
WORD

God is a promise keeper. I know this! But I would be lying if I told you that I've never wondered why He wasn't addressing my immediate need at that very moment. Then I'm reminded that I can't let my craving for instant gratification cause me to forget what He has said. His promise is, "Never will I leave you; never will I forsake you" (Hebrews 13:5).

While God doesn't work on my timeline, I know that He will come through for me. It is like a child taking the hand of a parent, trusting that where the parent leads is a wonderful place to go. And our wise heavenly Father knows when and where we are going, and He is much more capable than we are. We can take His hand, knowing that He is leading us moment by moment. He will always be with us because He always keeps His Word.

Do you ever have negative thoughts? With seventy thousand thoughts per day, I'm sure we all do.

As an artist, I'm often left alone with my thoughts, and for me, that's not always a good thing. I have a tendency to overanalyze everything. And when I started freelancing, I spent most of my days drawing, which gave my mind plenty of time to wander. Before I knew it, I was caught in my own downward spiral of negative thoughts: overthinking past events, pondering what others were thinking of me, and imagining what they might be saying behind my back... This was all dragging me down emotionally, and even worse, I was starting to believe some of my own lies that I concocted.

While our brain is an extraordinary organ, we need to keep it on track. The Bible reminds us of things we should focus on and think about: whatever is true, noble, right, pure, lovely, admirable, excellent, or praiseworthy (Philippians 4:8).

Take some time today to focus on the good things, the beautiful things, the excellent things. I hope you'll find, like I did, an inner peace and a better way of life.

ABOUT THE AUTHOR

Stefan Kunz was born into a missionary family in Africa, where he learned at an early age how to encourage those around him. Now as a talented artist, Stefan shares his heart and faith through his extraordinary artwork posted around the world. Stefan's hand lettering has captured the attention of clients such as Asics, Adobe, Apple, Coca-Cola and many more. Stefan is a modern-day, digital encouragement ninja, sharing the gospel and encouraging others and reaching hundreds of thousands of people with God's love.

Dear Friend,

This book was prayerfully crafted with you, the reader, in mind—every word, every sentence, every page—was thoughtfully written, designed, and packaged to encourage you...right where you are this very moment. At DaySpring, our vision is to see every person experience the life-changing message of God's love. So, as we worked through rough drafts, design changes, edits and details, we prayed for you to deeply experience His unfailing love, indescribable peace, and pure joy. It is our sincere hope that through these Truth-filled pages your heart will be blessed, knowing that God cares about you—your desires and disappointments, your challenges and dreams.

He knows. He cares. He loves you unconditionally.

BLESSINGS!
THE DAYSPRING BOOK TEAM

Additional copies of this book and
other DaySpring titles can be purchased
at fine bookstores everywhere.
Order online at dayspring.com
or
by phone at 1-877-751-4347